THE HEALTH CONSCIOUS LEADER

Protecting your visionary assignment
by making health a priority

THE VISIONARY LIBRARY BOOK 3

BY TONY ROGERS JR.

Copyright 2018 by Tony Rogers Jr.
Published by Visionary Press

No portion of this publication may be reproduced, stored in any electronic system or transmitted in any form or by any means, electronic, mechanical, photocopy, recording or otherwise, without written permission from the author. Brief quotations may be used in literary reviews.

Connect with Tony: thevisionarysocietyinfo@gmail.com

Contents

Introduction 1

Chapter 1 – The Power of Your Visionary Assignment 3

    Becoming a Visionary Leader 4

    Identifying Your Visionary Assignment 6

Chapter 2 – The Power of Health 9

    The High Cost of Putting Low Value on Your Health 9

    Getting Out of Your Own Way 11

Chapter 3 – The Mindset of a Health-Conscious Leader 13

    Three Beliefs of a Health-Conscious Leader 13

Conclusion 1

Resources for expanding your nutritional and fitness knowledge ....

Other books from the author ....

About the author ....

INTRODUCTION

Leadership is one of the most widely studied and documented topics on the market. There are scores of books published about this subject with dozens more written each year. So why write this book? Why do we need another one?

As you sift through the available literature on leadership, you'll begin to notice something is missing. There is much attention given to the indispensable qualities of great leaders such as character, communication, vision, and the like.

One equally important, yet often overlooked quality is that of sound physical health. I think we can agree that in the absence of good physical health, none of the other leadership qualities matter, which is why we must discuss this all-important issue.

This is not going to be your typical "health and fitness" book. I'm not going to tell you to count calories or lay off your favorite snacks (although those are not bad ideas). While these tidbits of information focus on the HOW-TO of health, that is usually not our problem. Most of us know the basics of good health but don't *apply* what we know because we don't have a strong enough WHY-TO. That is, we don't have a strong physiological driver pushing us to turn our health *knowledge* into health *habits*.

My goal with this short book is to provide that physiological driver by emphasizing one critical point:

The significance of your visionary assignment demands that your health become a priority.

Once you understand how significant your visionary assignment is to the world and how your health effects the execution of that assignment, you will naturally begin to make better health choices.

Chapter 1

The Power of Your Visionary Assignment

Leadership is the most important position on earth. No societal progress happens without a leader spearheading that change. Where there is no progress, there is no leader. And where there is no leader, there can be no progress. Leaders are often thought of as CEOs of large companies or people with distinguished corporate titles but neither of these are prerequisites for leadership.

What qualifies you to be leader? What initiates you into the ranks of visionary leadership? One word: responsibility. *The chief responsibility of a leader is to oversee and coordinate the transition of an intangible vision into a tangible reality.* In other words, the leader is in place to see that the original declared vision comes to fruition. Agreeing to take full responsibility for this transition is what qualifies a person to be called a leader. This agreement also marks the beginning of their visionary assignment.

These parameters dismiss the idea that only a select few of us were marked for leadership at birth while everyone else was destined to follow. *Everyone* has the capacity to lead in their own unique way and at different levels of influence. You only need to give yourself over to a cause bigger than yourself.

Becoming a Visionary Leader

The first book in The Visionary Library series is titled *Visionary: Making a difference in a world that needs YOU*. In that book, we dive deep into finding your purpose, writing a detailed description of your visionary assignment, and formulating a plan for its attainment. In this section, I want to briefly cover a few principles from that book pertaining to this topic.

The foundation of visionary leadership is finding a cause you want to lead. Finding a cause you want to lead is a matter of answering two questions:

- What world-problem do you want to help solve?
- What is your solution?

1. What world-problem do you want to help solve?

    Our world is broken and needs healing. Healing it is up to the visionary leaders and those who choose to join their initiatives. Doing your part in this healing process begins with deciding what problem you will help solve.

    Survey your environment and take notice of what problems stir up emotion in you. You probably already have an idea of what this could be. It's that reoccurring problem you think about throughout the day, the one that makes you angry when you or someone you care about experiences it. It's the injustice that makes you ask yourself, "Why hasn't anyone solved this?"

The problem that draws you to it may be isolated to your local neighborhood or it could be larger – even global in scale. Don't allow your mind to talk you out of trying because of the perceived size of the issue. There is a reason you are drawn to this particular world deficiency. It could be your calling to help solve it.

2. What is your solution?

Visionary leaders are solution-oriented individuals. They don't point out problems while casually waiting on someone else to fix them. They make a difference by providing clear, practical solutions to problems – solutions that other people can join them in implementing.

Now that you have an idea of what problem you want to help solve, the next step is coming up with a solution to that problem. The goal of your solution is a future where that problem no longer exists or the ongoing need is always met. Your vision is a description of how you will go about creating that change.

For example, let's say you've noticed a large gap in the resources available for young, inner-city men. You feel a deep need to help them navigate issues specific to their demographic. This is the problem you want to solve.

Your solution may be to form an after-school-and-weekend mentoring group specifically designed to tackle the needs of these young men. You may teach them the importance of education, community service, and other important qualities such as self-confidence, financial literacy, and entrepreneurship. This group may begin with a couple of students in your home and expand through word of mouth and marketing tactics campaigned in your local area.

This solution provides a clear path to how the original problem can be solved and a clear vision of how you could make a difference in the lives of those young men.

Identifying Your Visionary Assignment

Let's make this real by documenting your personal visionary assignment. Take out a clean sheet of paper and answer the following questions.

1. What world-problem would you like to help solve?

2. What is your vision for solving this problem?

3. Why does this cause matter to you? Why is it so important? Whom will it benefit? Who or what suffers if you do nothing? What hangs in the balance? Why must you act NOW?

After you answer each question, move on to the next chapter where you will find out how all this information relates to your physical health.

Points to Remember

1. Leadership is the most important position on earth. No societal progress happens without a leader spearheading that change.

2. The chief responsibility of a leader is to oversee and coordinate the transition of an intangible vision into a tangible reality.

3. The foundation of visionary leadership is finding a cause you want to lead. Finding a cause you want to lead is a matter of answering two questions:
   - What world-problem do you want to help solve?
   - What is your solution?

Chapter 2

The Power of Health

Various schools of thought exist around what good health is and how it is acquired. When I refer to health in this book, I'm referring to complete physical well-being, free of injury and disease.

As leaders, this must be our goal at all times because of the immense calling on our lives. Most people ignore their health until it is taken away. They fail to properly maintain the magnificent machine we call the human body until it breaks down. Not so for the visionary; we must be proactive instead of reactive when it comes to our health. For the sake of our assignment and the people that choose to join us on our journey, we need to place high priority on health.

The High Cost of Putting Low Value on Your Health

In the last chapter, I had you answer three questions to help identify your visionary assignment. I put special emphasis on the last question, which focused on the significance of your assignment because of its possible impact on your emotional state. I had you answer questions such as "Why is this cause so important to you?" and "Who or what suffers if you do nothing?"

My goal with these questions was to help you grasp the power and potential of your assignment. I want you to feel the full weight of your cause and realize how important you are to those whom your assignment affects. Doing this helps you realize that, because of your calling, your life is much bigger than you. The choices you make (including your health choices) could have a dire effect on a multitude of people.

I'll give you an example that really hit home for me. If you enjoy studying leadership, then you've probably heard of John Maxwell. He has written more than 30 books about leadership and is considered by many to be the Top Leadership Expert in America. Although John is obviously an excellent leader with a proven track record of success, he is still human and displays shortcomings as a leader, as we all do in certain aspects.

John struggles in the health department, specifically with keeping his health habits in check, which he candidly mentions in many of his books. His lack of self-discipline in this area almost cost him his life and could have meant the premature termination of his incredible vision.

According to his blog post titled "The Pain of Change," in 1998 while at a Christmas party he suffered a heart attack due to a small blood clot in his heart. Fortunately for John and his family, they were able to get him to the emergency room and perform surgery to remove the clot without any additional damage.

John further mentioned in the blog post that he's always been fond of eating rich foods such as steaks or chocolate cakes and wasn't one to exercise very much. He reported that since his heart attack, he isn't perfect, but takes his daily lifestyle choices and their consequences on his health much more seriously.

John's cardiologist gave him sage advice worth passing on here: "You help a lot of people and you are responsible for staying around as long as you can." These are words worth committing to memory whether you are a seasoned leader or just starting out on your visionary journey.

Getting Out of Your Own Way

John's situation is not an isolated event. These incidents happen all too often, many of them with fatal outcomes. Thousands of deaths each year are attributed to diseases and other conditions brought on primarily by lifestyle choices. This deeply saddens me – not only because of the obvious hurt it causes the victims' loved ones, but also the untapped potential that each person takes to the grave.

You must protect your vision from harm as you would anything else of great value. One of the ways you do this is by taking care of your health. When you don't make the right health choices, you are becoming your own enemy by essentially self-sabotaging your visionary assignment.

Every vision is naturally antagonistic to the current way of things, making it a target for naysayers and other obstacles hindering its ultimate execution. Don't add your health to the list of obstacles that stand in your way.

Points to Remember

1. Because of your calling, your life is much bigger than you. The choices you make (including your health choices) could have a dire effect on a multitude of people.

2. You must protect your vision from harm as you would anything else of great value. One of the ways you do this is by taking care of your health.

3. When you don't make the right health choices, you are becoming your own enemy by essentially self-sabotaging your visionary assignment.

Chapter 3

THE MINDSET OF A HEALTH-CONSCIOUS LEADER

Becoming a Health-Conscious Leader involves a fundamental shift in your mindset. One that requires you to view yourself as different from the masses. Throughout this book I've tried to facilitate this perceptual shift by helping you understand how important you are to the world.

In this chapter, I want to lay out the overall philosophy of a Health-Conscious Leader. I have divided the philosophy into three distinct beliefs that, when adopted, will help you live as a Health-Conscious Leader long-term.

Belief #1 – You are not normal.

The philosophy of the Health-Conscious Leader rests on the idea that you are not normal. You are an agent of change and have a special role to play in the advancement of our society. This mission isn't what makes you abnormal, because everyone has this same calling.

What makes you abnormal is that you have voluntarily decided to act on your unique way of fulfilling this calling. You have decided to believe in an invisible vision of a better future that no one can see but you.

There is no such thing as a "normal" visionary. Visionaries can be described with many words, but normal should never be one of them. Take pride in this fact and live your life like the agent of change you are.

Belief #2 – Good health is your duty.

Health-Conscious Leaders believe that doing what they can to maintain good health is their responsibility as a leader. This includes learning the basics of what it takes to live a healthy and fit lifestyle combined with consistently practicing this knowledge.

I want to stress here that this does not mean you need to be obsessed with adopting "special" diets or grow overly concerned about how much you exercise. It simply means that you will commit to living a reasonably healthy lifestyle complete with sensible eating habits and a good exercise regimen.

Focus on the consistency of your health habits and not so much on the intensity. Exercising for five hours, one day a week won't keep you fit but exercising for thirty minutes, four or five days a week will.

Belief #3 – Your body is your most important asset.

A Health-Conscious Leader knows that their body is their most important asset. It is the vehicle you were given to fulfill your visionary assignment. Your body is an incredible gift and you must not take it for granted. It gives you the ability to act on your ambitions and achieve your most highly-desired goals. The human body is extremely adaptive and resilient, yet it is still finite and can't go on forever.

Taking care of your body is not limited to exercise and nutrition. It also includes proper rest and stress management, especially for the hectic life of a leader.

Proper rest is one of the most important components of maintaining a healthy body. This is also the component of healthy living that I struggle with the most. I do my most creative work at night; it invigorates me to work on projects like this book that are directly tied to my visionary assignment. Either way, a major part of showing appreciation for my body is giving it the proper rest it needs to heal and revitalize itself. This is something I'm consciously aware of and have gotten better at over the years.

Good health is not given; it is earned. Some components of healthy living will come easily to you while others may not. Don't beat yourself up for this but also don't casually brush it off as unimportant. Continue to work on your health habits every day, knowing that over time you will be rewarded with the good health and longevity you have earned.

Points to Remember

1. Becoming a Health-Conscious Leader involves a fundamental shift in your mindset. One that requires you to view yourself as different from the masses.

2. The philosophy of the Health-Conscious Leader rests on the idea that you are not normal. You are an agent of change and have a special role to play in the advancement of our society.

3. Health-Conscious Leaders believe that doing what they can to maintain good health is their responsibility as a leader.

4. A Health-Conscious Leader knows that their body is their most important asset. It is the vehicle you were given to fulfill your visionary assignment.

Conclusion

Thank you for reading this book. My hope is that you have come to understand how valuable you are to the world and have been inspired to take control of your health habits. Good physical health is the engine of leadership, and the energy it generates is the fuel we use to make a difference.

OUR SOCIETY NEEDS YOU.
YOU HAVE AN ASSIGNMENT TO COMPLETE.
MAKE YOUR HEALTH A PRIORITY.

If this book has helped you in any way, please head over to Amazon.com and leave a review. I would love to hear your thoughts.

Recommended Resources for Expanding Your Nutritional and Fitness Knowledge

1. *The 7 Pillars of Health* by Dr. Don Colbert
2. *Eat to Live* by Dr. Joel Fuhrman
3. *Super Immunity* by Dr. Joel Fuhrman
4. *The China Study* by Dr. T Colin Campbell
5. *Fasting and Eating for Health* by Dr. Joel Fuhrman
6. *Prevent and Reverse Heart Disease* by Dr. Caldwell Esselstyn
7. *Bigger, Leaner, Stronger* by Michael Matthews

Other books from the author

The Visionary Library is an ongoing series of books dedicated to helping visionary thinkers create positive change in the world. You have just finished book #3 in this series.

Book #1 in this series is titled: *Visionary: Making a difference in a world that needs YOU*

Book #2 in this series is titled: *Writing to Make a Difference: How to share your message and secure your legacy by writing a nonfiction book.* You can find the entire series at Amazon.com

I also write about finances, relationships, weight loss, and other topics under the pen name Maurice Rogers Jr.

About the Author

Tony Rogers Jr. is an entrepreneur, teacher, and founder of The Visionary Society – a global training company dedicated to equipping visionaries with the tools and strategies they need to make a difference in the world. He is a proud native of Dayton, Ohio, the birthplace of aviation.